T0146706

The
Little Book
of Big Fun
Facts

The Little Book of Big Fun Facts

compiled and edited by

Lowell R. Torres

 iUniverse®

THE LITTLE BOOK OF BIG FUN FACTS

iUniverse books may be ordered through booksellers or by contacting:

iUniverse
1663 Liberty Drive
Bloomington, IN 47403
www.iuniverse.com
1-800-Authors (1-800-288-4677)

Because of the dynamic nature of the Internet, any web addresses or links contained in this book may have changed since publication and may no longer be valid. The views expressed in this work are solely those of the author and do not necessarily reflect the views of the publisher, and the publisher hereby disclaims any responsibility for them.

Any people depicted in stock imagery provided by Thinkstock are models, and such images are being used for illustrative purposes only. Certain stock imagery © Thinkstock.

ISBN: 978-1-5320-0231-1 (sc)
ISBN: 978-1-5320-0232-8 (e)

Print information available on the last page.

iUniverse rev. date: 07/07/2016

Contents

Preface

By the fall of 2004 I was growing sick and tired of college life. It had been three years and I was treading water, dissatisfied with my choice of History as a major but unsure of what, exactly I'd do with that when I graduated. I'd started college as a Journalism major but the rules were too confining and restrictive (a belief that would only be confirmed when I worked at the school newspaper a couple years later). So when an editor for the Indianapolis Star showed up to one of my J100 classes and said, "History majors end up as journalists as often as Journalism majors" I was at my advisor's office immediately to start the switch.

I didn't even really want to be a journalist, I just liked to – and wanted to – write. I wanted to be a novelist, to translate the stories that often popped into my head and took residence for a couple days or weeks or months or years. The problem was that I'd been hit by a nearly five-year-long bout of writer's block.

Oh I could write. I spent several years in the early 2000s writing on various new and fledgling versions of what would become the types of blogs that are common place today. I could write about sports, movies and TV shows, anecdotes about my life, or inane arguments about nothing in particular. What I could not do was write a single page of fiction.

Howard McMillen's creative writing class changed that. Howard was in his late 60s but a life of hard drinking made him look a decade older and the slight hints of dementia added to his aura. He ran the Wednesday night fiction writing class in an efficiently offhand way.

The first night of class he checked the attendance to the class roster then wrote the last name of each student on the board in groups of three. That, he explained, was the schedule. Produce at least 4 double-spaced pages on that date for him and every student in the class. The next week you'd have your story returned to you with his grade and everyone's critiques.

We would also spend a good 30-45 minutes discussing and constructively criticizing the works. My first two semesters in the class that time started with Howard, but as his affinity for going off into incoherent asides and random rambling increased so did our independence. By the third semester the students ran the class and the students who ran the class also happened to run the creative writing group on campus.

Within two more semesters I was the editor in chief of that group and was responsible for the production of The Tonic, the student literary magazine. To put it shortly, I loved doing that. I liked putting out the call for submissions. I liked reading the submissions. And I absolutely loved working on the design program and putting it together. I loved it so much that years later, when I found myself working at a self-publishing company who offered to let me publish two books a year for free, I used that opportunity to publish some more anthologies. *Hoosiers Writers* (Volumes 1 and 2) and *Zombies?! Zombies!!* were the first three productions of that benefit and you are now reading the fourth.

That's your first fact.

⌘

Anne Frank and Martin Luther King Jr were born in the same year but are known for two different eras in human history.

⌘

The University of Oxford was established earlier than the Aztec Empire.

⌘

Yoda and Miss Piggy are voiced by the same man, Frank Oz. He was also the original voice for Fozzie Bear and Animal as well as Bert, Grover and Cookie Monster. And he directed such movies as The Dark Crystal and Little Shop of Horrors.

⌘

One million seconds is a little over 11 days and one billion seconds is over 31 years.

⌘

When the oldest person on Earth was born, there was a completely different set of people on the planet.

⌘

In 2000 Blockbuster had the opportunity to buy Netflix for around $50 million. The company passed on the offer to instead make a deal with a subsidiary of energy giant Enron. The next year Enron went bankrupt. In 2013 Blockbuster made about $400 million in revenue. Netflix made $4.4 billion.

⌘

John Swartzwelder wrote 58 episodes of The Simpsons through its first fifteen seasons. Swartzwelder was also a chain smoker and would write his episodes in the same booth in his favorite diner. When California banned smoking in restaurants he bought the booth and had it installed in his home so he could continue to write in it.

⌘

Gene Reddenberry, creator of *Star Trek*, was asked about the casting of Jean-Luc Picard in *Star Trek: The Next Generation*. "Surely they would have cured baldness by the 24th century?" the reporter asked. Roddenberry replied, "In the 24th century, they wouldn't care."

⌘

An episode of the first season of the NBC series *Hannibal* featured a shot of a naked couple who had been flayed. This was deemed unacceptable by NBC, because the butt cracks of the couple were visible. The director compromised by filling the butt cracks with blood. NBC deemed it acceptable.

⌘

The first person to win the American version of *Who Wants to be a Millionaire* did so without using lifelines. He used his first and only lifeline to call his father and then told him he was about to win a million dollars.

⌘

Mr. Rogers made a point of mentioning out loud when he was feeding his fish after he got a letter from a family whose blind daughter asked him to do so, because she couldn't tell if the fish were being fed.

⌘

The scene in the movie "Spider-Man" where Peter Parker catches a falling Mary Jane and her tray of food contained no special effects. Director Sam Raimi shot the scene over and over again until actor Tobey Maguire managed to catch all the food, using only a sticky substance to keep the tray on Tobey's hand.

⌘

The original *Friday the 13th* was shot in New Jersey, and "Camp Crystal Lake" was and still is an active Boy Scout camp.

⌘

Samuel L Jackson's breakthrough role was playing a crack head in the movie *Jungle Fever*. He filmed the role two weeks after finishing rehab for crack addiction.

⌘

The 2002 movie *Spiderman* was the 5th highest grossing film of all time after its release. Over the past 12 years the movie has fallen to 49th.

⌘

The debut episode for both Wile E. Coyote and The Road Runner was titled, "Fast and Furry-ous."

⌘

In 2006 the Fox network aired a reality television program called *Unan1mous*. The purpose of the show was to lock 9 strangers in a bunker for an indefinite period of time, and they could only come out when they unanimously voted for the person among themselves who should be awarded $1,500,000. The award decreased with every day that passed and the eventual winner received $382,193.

⌘

The original Kermit the Frog was made from an old coat Jim Henson's mother threw out.

⌘

Freddie Prinze Jr. stepped away from acting in 2010 to become a writer and producer for WWE.

⌘

The actor who played the Green Power Ranger is a 7th degree black belt, professional MMA fighter and developed his own style of Karate.

⌘

In *The Jetsons* George Jetson was 40-years-old, Jane – his wife – was 33 and daughter

Judy was 16. This means they had Judy when George was 23 and Jane was 16.

⌘

William Shatner has appeared in a television show or movie every year since 1957.

⌘

Burger King's slogan for some TV commercials in the 90s was, "We're gonna make you love us."

⌘

Charlie Brown's little sister Sally was voiced by Fergie from the Black Eyed Peas throughout the 1980s.

⌘

The Comedy Central network showed only the message, "watching Johnny Carson's last show and so should you" during Carson's last *Tonight Show* broadcast.

⌘

DVD's of the Looney Tunes Golden Collection have a disclaimer explaining there were racial stereotypes in some of the cartoon shorts, but that airing them unedited, "would be the same as to claim these prejudices never existed."

⌘

Of the first 83 restaurants featured on *Kitchen Nightmares,* 50 have been sold or shut down.

⌘

Jim Cummings, the voice of Winnie the Pooh and (since 2000) Tigger, has worked with the Make-A-Wish Foundation to call sick children and talk to them in character.

⌘

WWE superstar John Cena has granted over 400 wishes for the Make-A-Wish foundation.

⌘

The 1982 horror movie *Poltergeist* used real skeletons as props because "they were cheaper than the plastic ones."

In August of 2001 actor James Woods was flying from Boston to Los Angeles and noticed four men acting suspiciously. He reported them but authorities never looked into his claim. They turned out to be four of the 9/11 hijackers.

In *First Blood* – also known as the first Rambo movie – the only death in the entire movie was an accident. Surprise might be understandable, seeing how 69 people die in the sequel, 132 die in *Rambo 3* and 236 in 2008's *Rambo*.

Employees at Disney who play Mickey Mouse must go through an autograph training session, as Mickey must have the same signature every time.

⌘

Walt Disney also liked to visit Disneyland incognito. He would wear old clothes and a straw farmer's hat, then ride the rides and time them to make sure they ran the correct amount of time.

⌘

It took 18 months to create the CGI Empire State Building in Peter Jackson's *King Kong*. The real Empire State Building only took 14 months to build.

⌘

A&W introduced a burger that was bigger and less expensive than McDonald's Quarter Pounder, but it failed because customers assumed 1/3 was less than 1/4.

⌘

On July 19, 1969, John Fairfax became the first person to row solo across an ocean. His fame, however, was short-lived as Neil

Armstrong and Buzz Aldrin landed on the Moon the very next day.

⌘

The US and Canada border is cleared for 20 feet so that no trees can grow . . . for all 5,000 miles.

⌘

Several studies have shown that standing like a superhero for as little as two minutes changes our testosterone and cortisol levels, increases our appetite for risk, causes us to perform better in job interviews, and generally configure our brains to cope well in stressful situations.

⌘

Since 1945 all British tanks have come equipped with the ability to make tea.

⌘

In Switzerland it is against the law to keep pet guinea pigs alone. A service even exists that provides a guinea pig companion to keep a lonely guinea pig company if its partner dies.

⌘

After a caterpillar creates a chrysalis, it dissolves into goo and then completely rebuilds itself into a butterfly.

⌘

The term "riding shotgun" originated in the old west. On a wagon or stagecoach, a person sat next to the driver and wielded a shotgun to scare or fight off thieves.

⌘

Pope Francis has Master's degrees in Chemistry, Philosophy and Theology from the University of Bueno Aires.

⌘

Alaska is the easternmost state in the United States, not Maine, due to the

Semisopochnoi Island being West of the 180-degree meridian.

⌘

Heels in shoes were first created by the Persian cavalry to keep stability while shooting arrows. It later became popular in Europe as a symbol of masculinity until 1630 when women's fashion trended towards masculinity.

⌘

Bessie Coleman was the first African American to hold an international pilot license. She had to learn to fly in France because no one would agree to train her in the US because of her gender and race. She was licensed two years before Amelia Earhart.

⌘

In an emergency coconut water can be used as a blood plasma.

⌘

A study showed that farmers who call their cows by name reported those cows producing 68 gallons more milk than those who did not.

⌘

Titanoboa was the largest snake that ever lived at over 40 feet long and 2,500 pounds.

⌘

It's been estimated that peeing in the shower can save up to 660 gallons of water per year, per person.

⌘

A single year on Pluto is longer than the whole history of the US. Pluto will complete its current rotation around the sun in 2030.

⌘

Thomas Edison sued his son, Thomas Edison Jr., to prevent him from using the family name after Junior endorsed several quack medicines and failed businesses.

⌘

Blue birds are blue due to structural refractory. Blue pigment is not possible from bird's dietary sources, so instead birds are blue for basically the same reason that the sky is blue.

⌘

The Plantaris is a small muscle in your calf that is believed to be used by our ancestors to grip with their feet. It is so weak that it is considered functionally obsolete and is absent in up to 10% of the population worldwide.

⌘

Spiders don't have muscles but instead control their blood pressure like a hydraulic system for movement.

⌘

The blue whale can produce the loudest sound of any animal. Its sound can be detected 500 miles away and is 188 decibels, louder than gunfire or a space shuttle launch.

⌘

Albert Einstein's brain has been rigorously examined over the years since his death. The most striking unusual feature of his brain is that he had an extra ridge on his mid-frontal lobe, the part of the brain used for working memory and making plans.

⌘

There is an island in Brazil where civilians are forbidden to go because it's overrun with snakes. There are up to 5 snakes per square meter over the entire island.

⌘

During the Battle of the Bulge an American paratrooper filled his helmet with beer from a destroyed pub and brought it to wounded soldiers in a nearby church. The story of him doing this became so famous in Bastogne that they have a local beer brand in his honor that even comes in helmet-shaped beer mugs in local pubs.

⌘

As of 2015, the last time the Chicago Cubs won a World Series was a month before Butch Cassidy and the Sundance Kid were killed in a shootout.

⌘

Shaquille O'Neal only made one three point shot during his entire career.

⌘

Actor Frank Welker has voiced the character Fred Jones in Scooby-do since the shows conception in 1969.

⌘

Alexander Graham Bell offered to sell his telephone patent to Western Union in 1876. They said no.

⌘

Rabbits can conceive a second litter before the first has been

⌘

In 1992 a storm caused 29,000 rubber ducks to be washed off a container ship and the knowledge gained from studying the duck's movements revolutionized our understanding of ocean currents. Many of the ducks are still believed to be floating around the world today.

⌘

Table knives, aka butter knives, have rounded tips because in 1669, Louis XIV decreed that all pointed knives be dulled down to reduce violence in Court and the streets.

⌘

Refried beans aren't fried twice or fried again. The "re" prefix comes from the

Spanish word "refritos" which means well-fried.

⌘

NASA has estimated the value of minerals in the asteroid belt as exceeding $600,000,000,000,000,000,000,000, or nearly $100 billion per person currently alive on earth.

⌘

Your tonsils can bounce higher than a rubber ball of the same size and weight, but only for the first 30 minutes after they've been removed.

⌘

The aardvark is the only species in its order. It is like no other animal on earth.

⌘

Baby elephants suck their trunks like human babies suck their thumbs.

⌘

Pom-pom crabs are named for their tendency to wave around stinging sea anemones in their claws to protect themselves against predators.

⌘

While most of the world's flowers and plants are pollinated by bees, cacao, which makes chocolate, is pollinated by a tiny fly from the same family as "no-see-um" flies.

⌘

The grasshopper mouse will howl like a little wolf to defend its territory.

⌘

Special breeds of rats have helped clear landmines in over 11 million square miles of Mozambique.

⌘

There was a song written in the 1630s that was performed only in the Sistine Chapel. The Vatican kept the composition secret for 150 years until 14-year-old Wolfgang Amadeus Mozart listened to the piece two times, transcribed it from memory, and produced the first unauthorized copy o the song.

⌘

American coinage was made using definite measurements. 16 pennies stacked equals 1 inch and 16 pennies in a line equals 1 foot.

⌘

Houston, Texas has a four-hour course that, upon completion, allows citizens to give tickets to those who abuse handicap parking spaces.

⌘

The rapper Nas listed his daughter as an executive producer on his Platinum album *Stillmatic*, so that they will always receive royalties from the album's sales.

⌘

Ray Bradbury originally titled his classic novel *Fahrenheit 451* as *The Fireman,* but he and his editors found the name to be boring, so they called a local fire station to ask what temperature book paper burned at. The firemen put Bradbury on hold, burnt a book, and reported that the book burned at a temperature of Fahrenheit 451.

⌘

During the Islamic Golden Age, scientists were paid the equivalent of what pro-athletes are paid today.

⌘

In 1940 twins were separated at birth and adopted by different families. Their families both named them James and as adults both would marry and divorce women named Linda, get remarried to women named Betty, have sons named James Allan and James Alan and dogs named Toy.

⌘

Hummingbirds will use spider silk to build their nests.

⌘

There is a town in Peru where men, women and children have fist-fights with each other on December 25, in order to settle old conflicts and begin the New Year with a clean slate. It's called Takanakuy.

⌘

The maggot was the first animal approved by the FDA as a medical device since maggots are very effective in cleaning dead tissue, disinfecting open wounds and stimulating healthy tissue growth.

⌘

In 2002 the Masai tribe of Kenya donated 14 cows to the United States to help with the aftermath of 9/11.

⌘

When news of the attack on Pearl Harbor arrived at Hitler's headquarters, one of the Nazi generals asked the rest of the group where Pearl Harbor was. No one was able to answer him and they had to consult a world map

⌘

The longest traffic jam in history so far occurred in China, was 62 miles and lasted 12 days.

⌘

The model for Uncle Sam on the famous poster from 1917 was the painter of the poster, James Montgomery Flagg. He aged his own portrait and added the goatee beard in order to avoid finding and hiring a model.

⌘

There is a phenomenon in England called the "halftime kettle effect" which happens during halftime of England's matches in the World Cup, when everyone rushes to run their tea kettles on before the game starts back up.

⌘

A registered nurse was watching the HGTV show *Flip or Flop* when she noticed a lump on the host's neck. She emailed the production company about her concern which prompted the host to get checked, and discover he had thyroid cancer.

⌘

On an 8x8 chessboard there are 26,534,728,821,064 ways for a knight to visit every square once and end up back at the square it started from.

⌘

In 1999 three suicide bombers exploded too soon because their bombs were set to daylight savings time.

⌘

Members of the band blink-182 once incorporated under the name Poo Poo Butt, LLC. because "it would be funny to have our accountants, managers and attorneys having to say that over the phone every day.

⌘

In the US all even numbered highways run east to west and all odd numbered highways run north to south.

⌘

In 47 seasons of existence, the San Antonio Spurs have missed the playoffs only 5 times.

⌘

The Venus flytrap is only found natively within a 60 mile radius of Wilmington, North Carolina.

⌘

During World War 2 most of the Norwegian Royal Family, including the current King of Norway, lived in the White House.

⌘

Fungi are more closely related to animals than they are to plants.

⌘

A carrot can trigger a touch screen, but only if held by a human.

⌘

The average female cat has one to eight kittens per litter and two to three litters per year. With a healthy productive life a single cat could have more than 100 kittens. A single pair of cats and their kittens can produce as many as 420,000 kittens in just seven years.

⌘

The kangaroo doesn't have many natural predators, mainly the dingo and humans.

One of their defensive tactics is to lead a pursuer into water where they will stand chest-deep and then drown their attacker.

⌘

Starfish don't have brains and have filtered seawater in their system instead of blood.

⌘

All modern pet chinchillas are descended from the twelve chinchillas that were caught in Chile in 1918 by Mathias Chapman.

⌘

Contrary to popular belief, goldfish have a memory that lasts three months or more. They can be trained to react to light signals and perform tricks.

⌘

The word robot comes from the word *robota*, which means "forced labor" in Czech.

⌘

Archaeologists in Denmark discovered a group of 700-year-old barrels that were used as latrines and were still full of the contents. They still stunk.

⌘

Coconut crabs can reach up to three feet in length, climb trees and have been observed eating chickens and cats. A group of them is called a nightmare.

⌘

3.2 billion people around the world watched the 2010 World Cup Final, or 46.4% of the entire global population.

⌘

A scientist at the University of Southern Mississippi developed a plastic that turns red when damaged. Putting it in sunlight or increasing the temperature then causes it do begin to heal itself in the same way as human skin.

⌘

Male fruit flies turn to alcohol when they are rejected by a female.

⌘

In the 1990s Pepsi and Russia struck a deal to bring Pepsi products into the country. As part of the deal Pepsi received 17 submarines, 10 commercial ships, a cruiser, a frigate and a destroyer. It gave Pepsi one of the more powerful naval fleets in the world, until they sold it for scrap.

⌘

A pound of dimes, quarters and half-dollars, in any combination, is worth $20.

⌘

KFC is such a popular Christmas dinner in Japan that it may be ordered up to two months in advance.

⌘

In the past hat-making involved prolonged exposure to mercury vapors; this caused poisoning with symptoms that included sensory impairment and lack of coordination. This is how the term "mad as a hatter" was created and inspiration for the Mad Hatter of *Alice in Wonderland*.

⌘

The term "Chinese Fire Drill" was coined after a British officer miscommunicated instructions to his Chinese crew during a fire drill. The result was that they pulled water from the starboard side of the ship and immediately dumped it over the port side, skipping the 'putting out the fire' part of the process.

⌘

India currently has more people using the internet than there are total people in the United Sates.

⌘

It's illegal to own hamsters as pets in Hawaii.

⌘

There is a type of food fraud where honey is cut with cheaper sugars and syrups, then sold as pure honey. It's called "Honey Laundering."

⌘

Poison dart frogs that are kept in captivity are not dangerously toxic due to the lack of alkaloids coming from their prey, which makes them poisonous. Bugs fed to them in captivity do not have these chemicals.

⌘

Three Gorges Dam in China has slowed the Earth's rotation by 0.06 microseconds.

⌘

Pears, apples, almonds, and other fruit are all members of the rose family; peanuts belong to the legume family with beans and peas; watermelon, cucumbers, and bananas are berries.

⌘

The Caribbean Taino natives believed in a deity called Guabancex, the goddess of chaos and destruction, who would call upon a storm called the "juracán". This is where the Spanish word "huracán" comes from, which later became the English word "hurricane"

⌘

The US Navy diving manual has detailed instructions for escaping a giant clam.

⌘

The highest paid athlete of all time is an ancient Roman charioteer named Gaius Appuleius Diocles, who earned the equivalent of $15 billion before his retirement.

⌘

A woman in Utah gave birth in 2004, 2008, and 2012, each year on February 29.

⌘

Until 2011 beer was classified in Russia not as an alcoholic beverage, but a soft drink.

⌘

In 2005 a glitch in the game World of Warcraft allowed a plague to spread throughout the virtual world. This led to non-infected players abandoning cities while the infected were forced into quarantines. The event was later studied by epidemiologists to see how people might react to a real life pandemic.

⌘

Your nose is always visible to you but your brain learns to ignore it through a process called Unconscious Selective Attention.

⌘

Harrison Ford has had a species of spider (Calponia harrisonfordi) and a species of ant (Pheidole harrisonordi) named after him for his conservation work.

⌘

Pound for pound, spider silk is stronger than steel.

⌘

If an elephant had the same metabolic rate as a shrew it would quickly overheat and explode.

⌘

Owen J. Baggett became a legend in World War II after his plane was badly hit and he shot down a Japanese fighter plane with his M1911 pistol, while parachuting to the ground.

⌘

Frozen pizza is so popular in Norway that when one of the major brands released a new jingle, it reached #1 on the Norwegian music charts.

⌘

Scientists studied an African Grey Parrot named Alex for 30 years and found he had the intelligence of a five-year-old human. He had a vocabulary of more than 100 words and could ask for a treats or to go to a different place. If he asked for a banana but was offered a nut instead, he would stare in silence, ask for the banana again, or take the nut and throw it at the researcher. Every night when his researchers would leave he would say, "You be good, see you tomorrow. I love you."

⌘

The artificial sweetener sucralose was discovered when a researcher misheard a command to "test this chemical" as "taste this chemical."

⌘

The metallic smell of money is actually the body oils on your fingers breaking down in the presence of iron or copper. You can see this by using a paper towel to pick up a penny and smelling it, then rub your fingers on it and smell again.

⌘

A feral pig once drank 18 cans of beer, fought a cow and then passed out drunk under a tree.

⌘

Millionaire Harris Rosen adopted an urban neighborhood in Florida, giving all families daycare, boosting the graduation rate by 75%, and cutting crime in half.

⌘

Tigers cannot purr so to show happiness they squint or close their eyes. Losing vision is lowering defense, so tigers only purposely do so when they feel comfortable and safe.

⌘

In Medieval France there was a legal category called "enbrotherment" that allowed two men to share living quarters, pool their resources and effectively live as a married couple.

⌘

Caribou, or reindeer, are the only mammals able to view the ultraviolet spectrum. This allows them to detect possible threats against the whiteness of snow.

⌘

"Quash" is a verb used to describe something being crushed in a non-physical sense, while "squash" is a verb used to describe something being crushed in a physical sense.

⌘

The Latin name for the American Plains bison is "Bison bison bison."

⌘

Prairie dogs have such a complex means of communication that they can embed descriptions of predators within their calls, and even have a call to describe a man with a gun.

⌘

Mathematician George Dantzig solved two of the most famous problems of statistics because he came into class too late to hear that they were supposed to be unsolvable.

⌘

Burger King introduced a Left-Handed Whopper in 1998 with all condiments rotated 180 degrees, which attracted thousands of customers.

⌘

The largest living organism on earth is a honey fungus measuring 2.4 miles across in the Blue Mountains of Oregon.

⌘

Mountain goats are not in the same genus as goats. They're part of the bovidae family, associated with antelopes, gazelles and cattle.

⌘

H	O	W							
			G	E	R	R	Y	-	
M	A	N	D	E	R	I	N	G	
				W	O	R	K	S	

50 precincts: 60% dark grey, 40% light grey

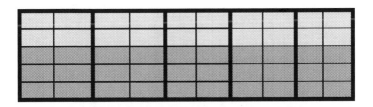

5 Districts: 5 Dark Grey, 0 Light Grey:
Dark Grey Wins

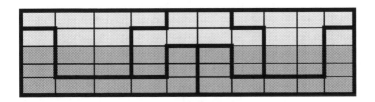

5 Districts – 3 Light Grey, 2 Dark Grey:
Light Grey Wins

Australia

An episode of the cartoon *Peppa Pig* was banned in Australia because it taught children not to be afraid of spiders.

⌘

Australia has the largest camel population in the world. Yes, Australia. The country saw a mass importation between 1860 and 1907 for use traveling. The large numbers were abandoned as autos gained popularity and they went wild. So wild that in 2009 a caravan of camels attacked and completely shut down the small outback town of Docker River.

⌘

In 1932 Australia fought a war, and lost, against emus.

⌘

The city of Melbourne, Australia was originally called Batmania after infamous explorer John Batman. His namesake still exists today in places such as Batman Avenue and the electoral division of Batman.

⌘

There is a pink lake in Australia called Lake Hillier.

⌘

There is a mountain in Australia called Mt. Disappointment. It was named such because the explorers who first reached the summit found the view to be subpar and wanted to reflect their feelings in the name they chose or the mountain.

⌘

Between 1932 and 1939 a man named Oskar Speck kayaked from Germany to Australia only to arrive and be detained as a POW due to the outbreak of World War 2.

⌘

There is a plant in Australia that will make you vomit in pure agony just by touching it.

⌘

In Australia torn bank notes are worth the portion of the note left, so half a $20 note is still worth $10.

⌘

The International Space Station has a faster internet speed than the average internet speed in Australia.

⌘

You are required to vote in Australia and will receive a fine if you don't.

⌘

In 1859 a man named Thomas Austin released 24 wild rabbits imported from England. By 1920 there were an estimated 10 billion rabbits in Australia.

⌘

The first commercial refrigerator was created by James Harrison, an Australian, in order to keep beer cool.

US Presidents

Benjamin Harrison was the first to have electricity in the White House. The 23rd president was unsure of this new technology, as he never touched any of the light switches for fear of being electrocuted.

⌘

When the Whiskey Rebellion happened in 1794, George Washington became the only sitting president to ever lead troops in the field.

⌘

Daniel Webster was never president, though he ran for the office three times and lost. Twice he was offered the Vice Presidency and twice he refused. Both times the president died in office, William Henry Harrison after just one month in office and Zachary Taylor after 16 months, meaning Webster could have been president. His reason for declining? He thought the office of VP would have made him irrelevant, "I do not propose to be buried until I am really dead and in my coffin."

When the President is unmarried or his wife dies during his term, another female relative becomes First Lady. Three president's daughters, two president's sisters, two nieces and two daughters-in-law have been First Lady.

President Canaan Banana was the first president of Zimbabwe.

Calvin Coolidge was known as "Silent Cal" for being a man of few words. A famous story example of this saw Coolidge seated at a dinner next to someone who said, "I made a bet today that I could get more than two words out of you." Coolidge responded, "You lose" and said nothing else the rest of the dinner.

⌘

Theodore Roosevelt could fill a book of fun facts alone – he had a black belt in jujitsu, was a champion boxer, kept a bear and hyena as pets at the White House, would ride his bike around New York City at night fighting crime as police commissioner - but for all his deeds and accomplishments he was like many fathers throughout history: he couldn't control his rowdy teenage daughter. Alice Roosevelt was known to smoke cigarettes, ride in cars with men, make bets with bookies, and stay out late partying while also frequently interrupting him in meetings to give him diplomatic advice. Roosevelt was quoted as telling someone who complained about his daughter, "I can be President of the United States or I can attend Alice. I cannot possibly do both."

⌘

Gerald Ford is the only man to serve as both Vice President and President without being elected to the office. Richard Nixon nominated Ford after VP Spiro Agnew resigned, and later when Nixon himself resigned Ford then took the office of President.

⌘

John Tyler was the 10th president of the United States, elected in 1790, and he has at least one grandson alive today. Tyler was 63 when he had a son who he named Lyon. Lyon would go on to have two children at 69 and 73, both of whom were alive, though one was ill, in 2012.

⌘

The United States hasn't had a president with a beard since 1893

⌘

The man who assassinated President James Garfield bought his gun based on how it would look in a museum exhibit.

It's also believed that Garfield would have survived the bullet wounds had more capable doctors treated him, as his doctors didn't believe in washing their hands or instruments before probing or attempting to operate. Garfield would suffer for two months from blood poisoning and infections before dying.

⌘

President James Buchanan regularly bought slaves and then granted them their freedom in the north.

⌘

Jimmy Carter was the first president to be born in a hospital.

⌘

Martin Van Buren was the first president to be born a US citizen (all the others were born before the Revolution) but also having grown up in a Dutch-speaking community, was the only president to speak English as a second language.

⌘

George W. Bush created the largest conservation area in the US and largest protected marine zone in the entire world.

⌘

President Andrew Jackson hated paper money and thought it was inherently evil, a device to make bankers rich and bilk farmers of their money. Jackson is now on the twenty-dollar bill.

⌘

More US presidents have died on the Fourth of July than any other day. James Monroe died in 1831 while Thomas Jefferson and John Adams both died on July 4, 1826.

⌘

George HW Bush was gifted a nine-foot-long Komodo dragon named Naga by the Indonesian government. He donated it to the Cincinnati Zoo.

⌘

George Washington was the owner and operator of the country's largest whiskey distillery when he was elected president.

⌘

Abraham Lincoln is the only US President to obtain a patent; he patented a type of flat-bottom boat used to transport goods downriver.

⌘

President Ulysses S. Grant smoked an estimated 12 cigars a day. Not coincidentally, he was the first president to die of cancer.

⌘

Woodrow Wilson is the only president to have earned a Ph.D., and the only political scientist to become president.

⌘

On Jimmy Carter's second day in office he pardoned hundreds of thousands of Vietnam War draft dodgers.

⌘

James Garfield could write well with both hands, at the same time, in English, Greek or Latin.

Ignaz Semmelweis

Ignaz Philipp Semmelweis was born on July 1, 1818 in what is now Budapest, Hungary. He came from a well-off family and studied law in Vienna in 1837 but later switched his focus to medicine, graduating with a specialization in midwifery in 1844.

As a doctor at Vienna General Hospital, Semmelweis grew concerned over the frequency of puerperal fever (also known as childbed fever) in new mothers which was resulting in a high mortality rate. After studying the issue, he discovered that the Vienna General Hospital operated two maternity clinics for different classes of patients. One clinic was staffed by medical students, the other by midwives, and soon he observed that the mortality rate was higher in the clinic with medical students. He couldn't figure out why.

Some time later a friend of his grew sick after surgery and died. Semmlweis performed the autopsy and discovered that the symptoms of the sickness were similar to his cases of childbed fever. And the surgery had been performed at a medical clinic similar to the one in his study. This led Semmelweis to declare that it was the medical students who carried infectious substances on their hands, as they would often go straight from dissecting cadavers to helping deliver babies. This also provided the logical explanation for the lower death rate in the second clinic operated by midwives, as they were not involved with autopsies or surgery.

Semmelweis took his results and initiated mandatory hand washing for any students or doctors treating his obstetrical patients. The application of this method instantly reduced the cases of fatal puerperal fever from 12 to 2%, and for the first time in the history of the hospital, there were some months with no deaths at all.

Ignaz Semmelweis helped usher in the antiseptic era of modern medicine.

The Human Body

⌘

If a pregnant woman were to suffer organ damage, the fetus can send stem cells to the damaged organ to help repair it.

⌘

Your heart rate automatically slows down when your face touches water. This is called the mammalian dive reflex.

⌘

When you're about to vomit and your mouth fills with saliva, this is your body trying to protect your mouth from the stomach acids in the vomit.

⌘

Those stomach acids? Strong enough to dissolve razor blades.

⌘

And that saliva? You produce about a pint of it a day.

⌘

The brain itself is incapable of physical pain.

⌘

You can always see your nose but you learn to ignore it.

⌘

Your forearm is the same length as your foot.

⌘

Every atom that is a part of you has been through the middle of a star.

⌘

About 7-10% of the population is missing the Plantaris muscle in their calf with no apparent ill effects. Surgeons often use it to replace or repair tendons elsewhere in the body.

⌘

Likewise about 15% of the population is missing the Palmaris longus in the wrist. You can tell if you have this by touching your pinky to your thumb; the muscle will appear as a straight line down the middle of your wrist.

⌘

A newborn baby is capable of hanging on a chin-up bar and supporting its own weight right after delivery, but loses the ability within hours and will not regain it for years.

⌘

Your taste buds have a lifespan of about 7-10 days, which is why you can burn your tongue and be able to taste things again a week later.

⌘

The brain operates on about the same amount of power as a 10-watt light bulb.

⌘

Some people can voluntarily move their tensor tympani muscle, located in the middle ear. This creates a sound like thunder or the ocean that only they can hear.

⌘

The ovaries and the Fallopian tubes aren't connected or even touching at all. After an egg develops in the ovary it shoots out towards the direction of the Fallopian tube, whose job is to catch the egg and move it down to the uterus.

⌘

The brain uses 20% of the total blood and oxygen in your body.

⌘

Your body's largest organ is the skin.

Printed in the United States
By Bookmasters